THE
Archive Photographs
SERIES

STOKE NEWINGTON

The Alexandra Theatre faces the police court across Stoke Newington Road in about 1910. Notice the elaborate lighting standard and the tram stop.

THE
Archive Photographs
SERIES

STOKE NEWINGTON

Compiled by
Gavin Smith

CHALFORD

First published 1995
Copyright © Gavin Smith, 1995

The Chalford Publishing Company
St Mary's Mill, Chalford,
Stroud, Gloucestershire, GL6 8NX

ISBN 0 7524 0159 9

Typesetting and origination by
The Chalford Publishing Company
Printed in Great Britain by
Redwood Books, Trowbridge

Reflections of Clissold House in the waters of the New River, 1905.

Contents

THE FOLLOWING ARMORIAL BEARINGS
were granted and assigned to the Mayor,
Aldermen and Councillors of the
METROPOLITAN BOROUGH OF STOKE NEWINGTON
by Letters Patent dated the 12th June, 1934

DESCRIPTION

ARMS : 1. The Crossed Swords and the red background represent the long connection of the Dean and Chapter of St. Paul's with Stoke Newington.
   2. The colour of the Cross is taken from the Arms of William Patten,
who rebuilt the old Church of St. Mary.
   3. The Oak Trees at the top of the Shield represent the ancient forest.
   4. The Lion (between the trees) is taken from the Arms of John Dudley.

CREST : 1. The Griffin is taken from the Arms ascribed to Daniel Defoe.
   2. The Banner held by the Griffin shows the Arms of Sir Thomas Abney.

The history of Stoke Newington in its coat of arms from a late 1930s Borough guidebook.

Introduction

There has been human activity in the Stoke Newington area from Stone Age times. Around Cazenove Road and Stoke Newington Common, particularly during housebuilding in the 1860s, archaeologists discovered a sequence of Palaeolithic tools. Pits, cellars, basements, and railway cuttings under construction yielded oval-shaped and pointed weapons, as well as scrapers, hammers, anvil stones, flakes, and cores. In Bayston Road pointed sticks from the same occupation were unearthed. This was the evidence left by early man of 200,000 years ago living on the banks of Hackney Brook.

Later, in Roman times, the very important road northwards, known as Ermine Street, left London via Bishopsgate and ran straight through the wild forest country of Kingsland, Shacklewell, Stoke Newington, and Stamford Hill. It later formed the eastern boundary of Stoke Newington Parish. In early records the name is rendered as Newtone, Newnton, and Stoke Neweton among other variants. It had a connection with the Dean and Chapter of St Paul's from Saxon times and it is believed that King Athelstane gave the manor to St Paul's in about 940 AD, leading to the parish being recorded as Neweton Canonicorum. The name Neweton came from its establishment as a new community inland won from the surrounding woodland. The forests of Middlesex and Essex were then vast tracts of forested country with many wild animals roaming around them.

As the community grew and prospered, important people found this a convenient retreat from the noise, dirt, and other dangers of London. Thus it was that Queen Elizabeth was believed to have visited the old manor house, next to the church. On the first occasion, when she was in danger from her sister Mary I's jealousy, it provided a safe haven out of sight of those wishing her harm. This connection led to the naming of a path behind the manor – Queen Elizabeth's Walk – which is the name it still holds today.

When James I of England came down from Scotland to claim the English throne, he was met at Stamford Hill by the Lord Mayor and Sheriffs of the City with great pomp, on 7 May 1603. Celebrating this event, the Cock and Hoop public house at the corner of Church Street and High Street changed its name to the Three Crowns, symbolising the new union.

At the beginning of the eighteenth century the Parish Field at the southern end of Stoke Newington was used to build houses for religious refugees from the Palatinate – thus the name Palatine Road. The estate formed a charity the proceeds of which went to St Mary's which was later divided among the daughter churches of the parish. Palatine House afterwards built on some of this land was frequently visited by John Wesley, when he needed rest and quiet from his preaching and other activities. During the eighteenth and nineteenth centuries many houses were built around the village for Nonconformists who were not permitted in London – thus famous people such as Isaac Watts and Daniel Defoe came to be associated with the village. Schools set up by this community proved to be excellent training places for many who were later to become famous in various fields. Defoe attended a school in Newington Green, and Edgar Allen Poe spent some time at a school in Church Street.

The City itself began to reach out its fingers of development in the nineteenth century, but the pace of life in the village was for a long time very gentle and descriptions of the area at this time stress its peace and tranquillity. Development eventually speeded up and gradually all the easier sites on the gravel and brickearth areas had been developed – the famous builder Cubitt cut his teeth as a mass provider of housing with projects around Albion Road.

Eventually, even the less easy clay soil began to fill up with new roads. In spite of all this Stoke Newington long retained an individuality, assisted by the retention of open areas such as Clissold Park, Abney Cemetery, and the Reservoirs, as well as the remaining houses from a more gracious age.

One
Along the Roman Road

Kingsland Chapel in the Olden Days.

Kingsland Chapel, an ancient building on the line of Ermine Street, the former main Roman Road to Lincoln and York, by way of Bishopsgate, Kingsland, Stoke Newington Road, and High Street and Stamford Hill.

Dalston Junction Corner on this High Road, looking towards London. The Crown and Castle are on the left and Balls Pond Road is to the left.

Left: The Welsh Chapel, Barretts Grove, off Stoke Newington Road going north. In 1906 this was the centre of a small Welsh community. Right: Leonard Huggett, Opticians, 9 Stoke Newington Road. The advert is a shrewd appeal to parents' aspirations for their children.

The Alexandra Theatre area of Stoke Newington in 1906.

The opening advertisement for the theatre, 1897.

Palatine House was built in the eighteenth century and looked like this in 1915. It had given shelter to John Wesley at a difficult time in his life in the 1780s. The name is explained in the introduction.

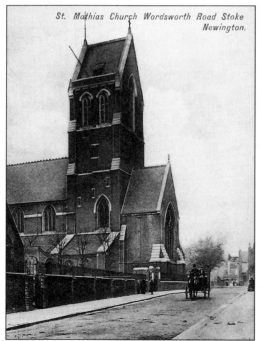

St. Mathias Church Wordsworth Road Stoke Newington.

Left: In 1906 St Mathias dominated Wordsworth Road, earlier known as Cut Throat Lane when it was a footpath in the fields from Newington to Shacklewell. Right: The other side of St Mathias from Goldsmith Square – the impetus for a new church at this end of the borough (Old St Mary's then the only one in the parish) was the idea of a devout layman, Robert Brett.

St Mathias in July 1853 – a view from the fields behind Balls Pond Road, from an oil painting. The vestry of St Mary's was mostly against a new church.

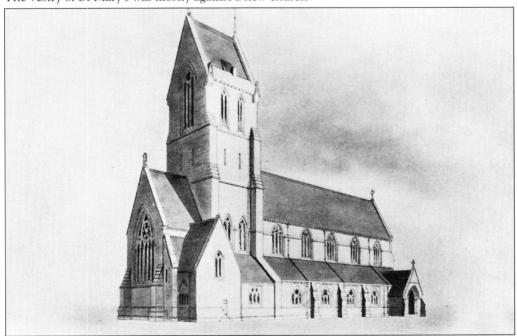

The famous architect Butterfield's drawing of the new St Mathias. In spite of opposition, Robert Brett brought together a team of supporters and benefactors and the church was opened in June 1853.

A quiet corner of St Mathias' parish. The sweet-smelling fields had given way to a mass of housing, some of it very poor.

A scene in Stoke Newington Road, full of movement. The electric tram and the pawnbroker's establishment on the corner of Wellington Road on the right were the ingredients of everyday life in 1907.

The shops by West Hackney Church, on the east side of Stoke Newington Road. Note the gaslit globes outside two of the shops.

A closer view of West Hackney Church on the corner of Amhurst Road, with the beginning of High Street in the distance, 1904.

Evering Road, one of the streets on the east side of the High Road. These neat residential streets are part of the Stoke Newington community although officially part of Hackney.

We are now in Stoke Newington High Street, with the police station on the left, and a Shoreditch-bound tramcar, 1911.

105. High Street, Stoke Newington.

A policeman stands on the step of the police station as an Edwardian tide of humanity swirls past.

1315   The Fire Station, High St., Stoke Newington

The impressive Victorian fire-station in what was described as the High Street but was actually tucked away in Leswin Road, just off the main thoroughfare, 1905.

A fine window display by George Sampson, retailer of hats and umbrellas, at 152 High Street.

A 1905 scene in the High Street. The entrance to Church Street by the Three Crowns Inn is in front of the horse bus on the left, with indicator notices for Kingsland Road and London Bridge.

Closer to the corner of Church Street, the High Street pavement on the right is dangerously overcrowded within its narrow confines. Above the shops are the rooms of Mr Pentney, Surgeon Dentist.

Rectory Road respectability, 1906. The dress of the people is very proper and so is the furnishing of the windows with their various styles of curtains and blinds.

Treescape, looking towards the church, Rectory Road, 1904. This important street connected Northwold Road and Shaclewell Lane parallel with the High Street on its east side.

Rectory Road Station, on the platform. Placards proclaim news from the Russo–Japanese conflict.

A drawing of the once-fashionable house at 187 High Street, occupied in 1937 by the Home Hospital for women.

Walter Mitchell's Tailors of 211 High Street is in this block on the left. The shops which are sited just before Abney Park Cemetery main entrance include Burr's Library, the Express coffee and dining rooms, and Dunkley, monumental masons.

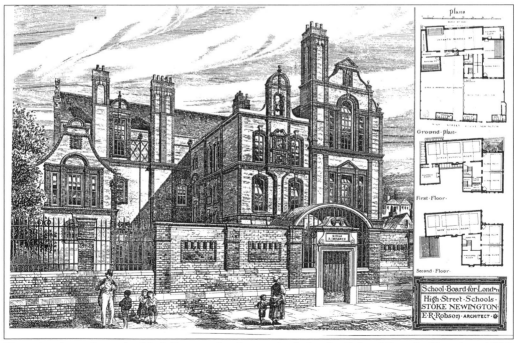

Opposite these shops the High Street schools were built for the School Board of London, 1876.

Rails and trees on Stoke Newington Common, 1905.

Northwold Road School at the bend in the road, 1905.

A horse-bus about to set out for the City from Stoke Newington Common. Even in 1908 there were traffic jams in London.

A crowd of children watch the photographer take a shot of St Michael's and All Angels, Stoke Newington Common.

A different angle shows the neighbouring streets by the church in 1910.

No. 22 Benthal Road, off Northwold Road, in 1907. Note the tiled path with a coal cover for deliveries to the cellar, also a step to the front door with an air vent underneath. There are marble door pillars, iron window bay supports, and different patterned courses decorating the elevation. This very respectable house is also equipped with neat iron railings, a gate, and stuccoed window surrounds in addition to the owner's smart net curtains and blinds. It is in this very area of the town that the stone implements of the inhabitants of 200,000 years ago have been found.

Osbaldeston Road with its leafy saplings, 1906.

The downward curve of Kyverdale Road, viewed from Cazenove Road in 1906.

The main gates of Abney Park Cemetery on the High Street, 1906. So many interesting trees were planted in its grounds that it at one time contained more specimens than Kew. It is now partly a natural history reserve.

The Weavers Arms, across from the Cemetery, and other shops mark the beginning of Stamford Hill, 1907.

LONDON. Cazenove Road, Clapton. No. 1105.

This splendid boulevard effect in Cazenove Road in 1920 resembles a continental location.

Stoke Newington station's low buildings set above the cutting make a dramatic contrast with the neighbouring parade of shops still intact today. The scene is from 1905.

Stamford Hill's impressively wide roadway and pavement area climb northwards past the parades of fine shops, 1903.

The Metropolitan Electric Tramway terminus at Stamford Hill in 1906.

Looking down from the terminus, 1906.

A Hackney Council watercart lays the dust in West Bank, Stamford Hill, as ladies and children promenade, 1910.

The wide curve of Amhurst Park at the northern edge of Stoke Newington, 1908.

The twin peaks of 77 Bethune Road, a double-fronted house with some pretension. The iron railings of the inner parts of the borough are here replaced by wooden fences and gateposts. Presumably, servants occupied these attic rooms in 1913.

CLAPTON BAKERIES · The *Summit* Shoe Co. · TOILET SPECIALISTS · Boots · DISPENSING CHEMISTS

The Broadway, Stamford Hill. N.16.   115262.

The excellent Broadway shopping area of Stamford Hill in the 1920s served the northern parts of Stoke Newington. The multiple shops such as Boots the Chemists and A.B.C. tea rooms share the parade with local firms like Clapton Bakeries. A sign illuminated at night indicates the Stamford Hill Cinema.

Two
Church Street
and St Mary's

Stoke Newington from the north west in about 1750, based on Chatelain.

The Three Crowns Inn at the corner of Church Street, 1903. The Stamford Hill and Holborn Horse Tram is just passing the spot. The competition between the trams and buses is quite hectic. Church Street developed on the ridge of high ground leading away westwards, from an early period of history. The Saxons gave the place its name of Newington, which was supplemented by the prefix Stoke in the Medieval period.

Fleetwood House was built in the 1630s, altered several times in the eighteenth century, and finally replaced in 1872 by Fleetwood Street, a Victorian development. A watercolour by T.H. Shepherd.

Another view of Fleetwood House in 1843 by T.H. Shepherd. A local resident, James Brown, commissioned T.H. and his son F.N. to record old Stoke Newington before it disappeared.

Interesting plaster panels from old Fleetwood House, which were preserved when it was demolished.

Abney House, the next great house westwards along Church Street, was recorded by T.H. Shepherd in 1843. It was the impending demolition of this building that prompted Brown to have drawings made of the old village.

Staircase and hall at Abney House. The building was begun in about 1690 by Thomas Gunston, a dissenting merchant. Dissenters were not allowed to settle in the City of London.

Workmen taking out the panelling from Isaac Watts' bedchamber, Abney House. When Gunston died in 1700, his sister, wife of Sir Thomas Abney, another Dissenting merchant and Lord Mayor of London in 1700, inherited the house. When widowed in 1722, Lady Abney moved in, bringing with her the famous Dissenting divine Dr Isaac Watts.

STOKE NEWINGTON. — ABNEY PARK CEMETERY.

Abney House gave way to a cemetery, meant to be non-denominational, but which was to become the resting place of leading Nonconformists, General Booth and other Salvationists. This open perspective of 1904 has given way to the present wooded appearance.

This mid-Victorian engraving shows the memorial to Dr Isaac Watts and the Chapel.

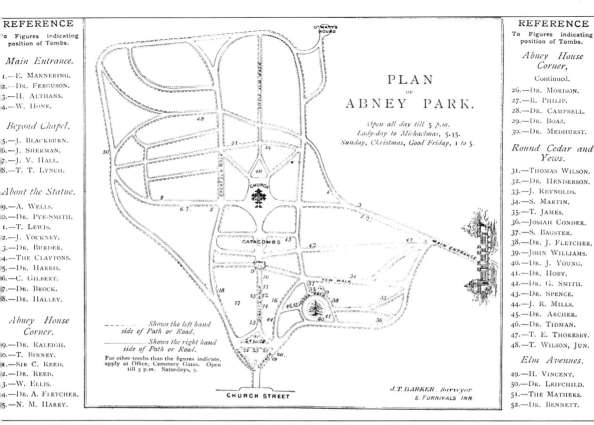

PLAN
OF
ABNEY PARK.

Open all day till 5 p.m.
Lady-day to Michaelmas, 5.15.
Sunday, Christmas, Good Friday, 1 to 5.

CHURCH

CATACOMBS

MAIN ENTRANCE

YEW WALK

- - - - - *Shows the left hand side of Path or Road.*
.... *Shows the right hand side of Path or Road.*

For other tombs than the figures indicate, apply at Office, Cemetery Gates. Open till 5 p.m. Saturdays, 3.

CHURCH STREET

J. T. BARKER, Surveyor
8, FURNIVALS INN.

Plan of the cemetery from a guide of 1833, *Walks in Abney Park*, when cemetery visiting was a Sunday leisure activity. Secular pleasures were frowned upon as a way of passing the Sabbath.

ABNEY PARK CEMETERY COMPANY, LIMITED.

Abney Park Cemetery,
STOKE NEWINGTON, N.

Chingford Mount Cemetery,
CHINGFORD, ESSEX.

GARDENING.

The Company's Charges are as follows :—

	Private Grave with Kerbs.			Private Grave without Kerbs.			Single Vault.			Double Vault.		
	£	s.	d.	£	s.	d.	£	s.	d.	£	s.	d
Planting with Flowers and Shrubs, according to Season, and maintaining for one year *⁎*	1	1	0	1	6	0	2	2	0	3	3	0
Planting with Shrubs only, and maintaining for one year ...	0	10	6	0	15	6	1	1	0	1	11	6
Turfing and keeping in neat order for one year	0	10	6	0	12	6	0	15	0	1	1	0
Planting with Shrubs only once ...	0	5	0	0	5	0	0	10	6	0	15	6
Turfing	0	2	6	0	2	6	0	5	0	0	7	6
Moulding	0	2	6	0	2	6	0	7	6	0	10	6
Banking	...		...	0	2	6	...		...	...		...

N.B.—The above charges apply to Graves and Vaults of the usual sizes. The planting of larger areas, or in special manner, may be arranged for with the Secretary.

Orders accompanied by a remittance will have the earliest possible attention. Contracts date from the 1st of the month of payment.

⁎ The Stones on Graves maintained with Flowers and Shrubs are kept in an upright position without extra charge.

2000. 5-94.   Waterlow & Sons Limited, Printers, London Wall, London.

Charges for gardening at the Cemetery in 1894.

A backward glance at Church Street in 1920. The classical pillars of Abney Chapel can be seen on the right, opposite the back wall of Abney Park Cemetery on the left in the middle distance.

toke-Newington. No. 1899.

Other interesting frontages of houses are in the right foreground. A Victorian shopping parade
occupies the left foreground.

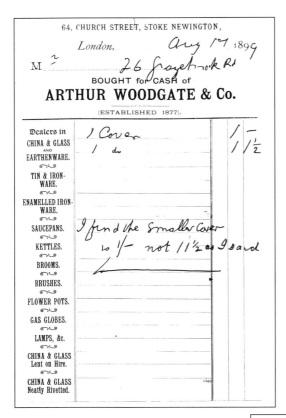

64, CHURCH STREET, STOKE NEWINGTON,

London, *Aug 17 1899*

M ² *26 Grazebrook Rd*

BOUGHT for CASH of

ARTHUR WOODGATE & Co.

(ESTABLISHED 1877).

Dealers in CHINA & GLASS AND EARTHENWARE.	1 Cover	1 / —
	1 do	1 / 1½
TIN & IRON-WARE.		
ENAMELLED IRON-WARE.		
SAUCEPANS.	*I find the smaller Cover*	
KETTLES.	*is 1/- not 1½ as I said*	
BROOMS.		
BRUSHES.		
FLOWER POTS.		
GAS GLOBES.		
LAMPS, &c.		
CHINA & GLASS Lent on Hire.		
CHINA & GLASS Neatly Rivetted.	1249	

Local tradesmen's bills from the 1890s.

M *26 Grazebrook*

Bought of W. & F. BURNINGHAM,

HIGH-CLASS

Cheesemongers, Poulterers & Pork Butchers,

20, CHURCH STREET, Stoke Newington,

AND

122, SEVEN SISTERS' ROAD, N.

Dec 18 1896

1/-

The Falcon Tavern in 1844 by T.H. Shepherd.

Leather warehouse in Church Street, 1893.

Daniel Defoe, often called the first novelist, came to reside in Church Street, Stoke Newington, from 1709–1729. Here, the immortal *Robinson Crusoe* was penned. It was also probably the first serialised publication.

A drawing of Defoe's house in Church Street. Seven years after coming to live in the village, he built 'A large house on the south side ... Square in plan ... it had deep window seats, curious cupboards in recesses, and massive bolts and locks ... '.

John Howard, the philanthropist and prison reformer (1726–90), from an impression of his statue in St Paul's. While travelling abroad he was unfortunate enough to be thrown in prison. Having been appalled by the conditions in which he was kept, he vowed to fight to reform British prisons. He lived in the old houses on the site of the Town Hall.

No. 122 CHURCH STREET, STOKE NEWINGTON.

Approaching the ancient Red Lion on a triangular piece of land by the junction with Lordship Road, and Red Lion Lane, it was once called the Green Dragon. Behind it were formerly the parish cage or gaol, the stocks, the whipping post, and the pound.

This picture of No. 109 Church Street, showing a survivor of the elegant houses that once lined this street, was painted by T.H. Shepherd in the 1840s.

CHURCH STREET, STOKE NEWINGTON.

Nº176.

Thriving Church Street in the mid-1920's, with the pavements thronged with shoppers. The Public Library had been opened in 1892. The white building is the War Memorial entrance of 1923.

MEMORIAL HALL, STOKE NEWINGTON.

Nº197.

The War Memorial and the corner of Edwards Lane are seen on the left with the tower of the new St Mary's Church in the distance.

LONDON. Church Street, Stoke Newington. No. 1005.

Looking beyond the ivy-clad walls of the library, the gateposts of the old houses in Church Row are visible. Here, many of Stoke Newington's famous people lived.

Mrs Barbauld was a very famous literary hostess and writer of her day – much admired for her writing skills. Her husband became 'morning preacher' at the chapel in Newington Green. To Stoke Newington to visit her came friends such as Charles Lamb, Wordsworth, Southey, Walter Scott, Hannah Moore, and Miss Edgworth.

By Church House, 1906.

To Church Row came Dickens, Wilkie Collins, and others from the world of the arts. Here they are in the garden of F.M. Evans, proprietor of *Punch* magazine, in an early photograph.

Halstead House and other old residences before demolition work in 1930 to prepare the site for the new Town Hall (Hanslip Fletcher drawing).

1518. OLD HOUSES, CHURCH ST., STOKE NEWINGTON.

Another view of old houses near the church, 1906.

Old St Mary's Church at the end of the eighteenth century.

The winding pathway through old St Mary's churchyard, 1905.

Old St Mary's Rectory in 1853. The new parish church of St Mary's was erected on the site and grounds of this old building and consecrated in 1858.

The staff of St Mary's parish churches.

The spacious interior of the new St Mary's at the beginning of the twentieth century.

The exterior of St Mary's Church of 1858 designed by Sir Gilbert Scott. The spire was not added until 1890, the work of his son J. Oldrid Scott. In the background of this picture, work is going forward on the new Town Hall.

Looking past Kennaway Hall and Paradise Row to the spire of the new church, 1906.

The gates of Paradise House School, 1920.

Schoolboys and schoolgirls outside Paradise House in 1905.

The playground of Paradise House School in 1920.

Kennaway Hall, Paradise Row, in the 1920s. This building became a Church Missionary Training Home in 1937.

Netball at Kennaway Hall.

Kennaway Hall Dining Room.

The entrance hall of Kennaway Hall.

Evolution of the English Noah's Ark in Stoke Newington

Born in February 1915 in a Carpenter's Workshop lent by a Borough Councillor, **WAR RELIEF TOY WORK** was organized to give employment to the Invalid and Old who were thrown out of work.

During the War Years it was financed by the Borough **WAR RELIEF** (Civilian) **FUND**. But when moved in 1916 over the War Pensions Offices, its scope was extended to disabled ex-Service Men and their Dependants, who ever since have been the chief employees—all of whom are more or less physically unfit.

Noah's Arks have always been the speciality of the Industry. Stoke Newington might well be proud of the place they have gradually gained in the World's Market—through design and workmanship.

Every ark carries a reminder of God to the children in the Nursery rhyme inside the lid.

Particulars if desired from Honorary Manager—

WAR RELIEF TOY WORK
WARWICK HOUSE
255 STOKE NEWINGTON CHURCH STREET, N.16

Registered under the War Charities Act, 1916.

War Relief toy work at Warwick House, next to Kennaway Hall in Paradise Row.

MANSION, NEWINGTON

Residence of the late Crawshay Esq.

An early impression of Clissold House, designed by Joseph Woods about 1790, from across the New River in the Paradise Row area.

Looking down Clissold Road from the Park End in 1906.

Paradise in Stoke Newington – the Row and the River.

Three
North of Church Street

Queen Elizabeth's Gate at Newington.

The remains of Queen Elizabeth's Gate behind the old Manor House, Church Street, at the end of the eighteenth century.

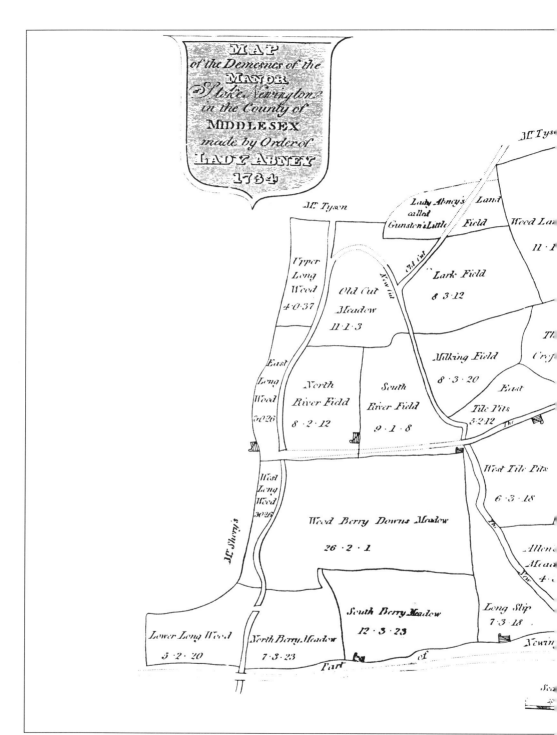

This map of the demesne lands of the Manor show the manor buildings on Church Street at the right-hand side. The fields and features between it and Woodberry Down are given in detail with the field gates marked, 1784.

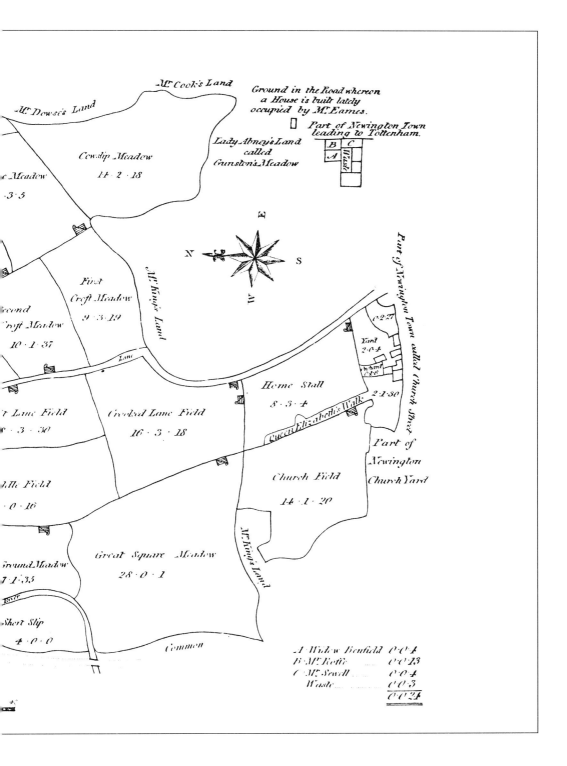

Mr Cook's Land

Mr Dowse's Land

Ground in the Road whereon a House is built lately occupied by Mr Eames.

Lady Abney's Land called Gunston's Meadow

Part of Newington Town leading to Tottenham.

B C
A Walk

Cowslip Meadow
14 · 2 · 18

Meadow
· 3 · 5

E
N · · S
W

First Croft Meadow
9 · 3 · 19

Mr King's Land

Second Croft Meadow
10 · 1 · 37

Lane

0 · 2 · 7

Yard
2 · 0 · 4

Home Stall
8 · 3 · 4

2 · 1 · 30

Queen Elizabeth's Walk

Part of Newington Town called Church Street

Lane Field
· 3 · 30

Crooked Lane Field
16 · 3 · 18

Church Field
14 · 1 · 20

Part of Newington Church Yard

le Field
· 0 · 16

Great Square Meadow
28 · 0 · 1

Mr King's Land

Ground Meadow
· 1 · 35

Short Slip
4 · 0 · 0

Common

A Widow Benfield   0 · 0 · 4
B Mr Rotte   0 · 0 · 13
C Mr Sewell   0 · 0 · 4
  Waste   0 · 0 · 3
                    ————
                    0 · 0 · 24

Courtiers ride through Queen Elizabeth's Gate at the start of a day's field sport – the dogs and falcons/hawks await the hunters. An imaginative reconstruction of a scene from the Middle Ages by F.N. Shepherd.

Houses in Queen Elizabeth's Walk, 1903.

No. 124 QUEEN ELAZABETH'S WALK, STOKE NEWINGTON.

The park side of Queen Elizabeth's Walk at its southern end, 1903.

As building operations began to accelerate in the mid-Victorian era, Queen Elizabeth's Walk was extended northwards and villas and houses were constructed in different styles along its length. This is No. 51 in 1908.

Mrs Evans with her child outside No. 21 Allerton Road. By the end of the nineteenth century, houses filled this road just south of the waterworks and reservoirs. The bay windows and doorways with their ornamentation can be glimpsed. There was a marble step up to the doorway with a coal cellar extending back, underneath.

Looking west along Allerton Road from the front garden of No. 21. The houses had a small front garden with lawns and flowers and trees or a hedge inside the front wall with its railings. The inside layout of No. 21 was curious, with upper half floors with two or three rooms each (the back portions of the houses were slightly lower than the front) and a low-ceilinged top floor.

A horse bus emerges from Lordship Park between the heraldic pillars marking its entrance. There is a glimpse of the large houses in Green Lanes, Brownswood Park. Green Lanes runs across this view from 1908.

LORDSHIP ROAD, STOKE NEWINGTON.

These houses in Lordship Road, seen in 1912, were built along what was once a drovers' route from north to south through the fields, continuing via Cut Throat Lane to Kingsland and Dalston on the road to London.

Looking from the corner of Lordship Park in 1904. Lordship Road runs northwards towards the reservoirs. Manor Road Presbyterian Church, on the right, always numbered expatriate Scots in the congregation. This church continued Stoke Newington's Nonconformist traditions.

Further along Lordship Road in 1912, the villas are set behind generous gardens. For much of the day, the only sound was birdsong or the rumbling passage of a horse and cart.

The continuation of Lordship Park is Manor Road. A horse bus on its way to Stoke Newington station is the only vehicle to be seen. This form of transport disappeared in 1907.

1021. Fairholt Road, Stoke Newington.

Fairholt Road, one of the byways marching towards Stamford Hill in 1908.

New River Woodberry Down

The Bungalow.

The New River at Woodberry Down. The cottage has been labelled as 'the bungalow' – though not of the accepted one-storey type. The date is 1909.

Water Board employees on the bank of the New River, 1912. Constructed between 1609 and 1614 by the entrepreneur Sir Hugh Myddleton with patronage from King James I, its object was to provide the City of London with a reliable fresh water supply.

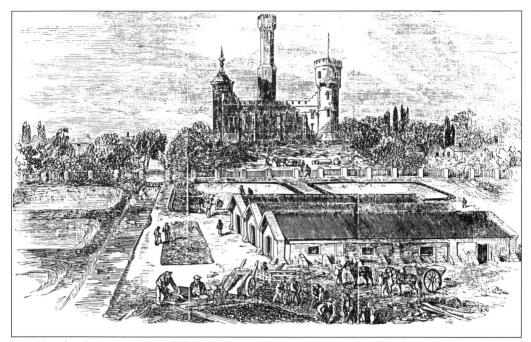

In 1830, the Company created the Stoke Newington reservoirs by filling in two old gravel pits. The banks were faced with stone from the demolition of old London Bridge. After cholera epidemics, new rules for domestic water supply led to the laying out of filter beds across Green Lanes and the erecting of the pumping station.

1493 The Reservoir.

Water-babies enjoy their unique play area outside their cottages, 1910. A number of employees of the Water Board lived on the banks of the New River and the reservoirs.

Another view of the river, reservoirs, and cottage by Lordship Road Bridge. The area became popularly known as the 'Lake District of North London'.

The engine-house, Lordship Road, about 1903.

Cintra Cottage, Stoke Newington.

An early nineteenth-century engraving of Cintra Cottage, which faced the junction of Lordship Road with Woodberry Down.

Four
Clissold Park

Clissold Park, Stoke Newington. No. 1846.

The bandstand area of Clissold Park, 1905. The park of fifty-four acres was opened to the public in 1889, the Earl of Rosebery performing the ceremonial act.

CLISSOLD PARK, (Photographed from an Aeroplane.)

An aerial view of Clissold Park, 1905, produced by the local firm Aero Photo Co of 54 Bouverie Road when such things were still pioneering wonders and the photographer had to take his life in his hands, balancing his heavy apparatus on the edge of the cockpit. The boundary of the park with Queen Elizabeth's Walk can be seen in the far distance.

Clissold Park Lodge at the North Western entrance, 1906. During the first half of the twentieth century, London parks were staffed by 'parkies' who kept in check the worst excesses of children let loose in areas of their jurisdiction. The 'parkies' wore a darkish brown uniform and many lived in lodges such as these adjacent to the place of their duties.

Deer in their pen with Clissold House beyond, 1905. From its early days as a park the authorities encouraged the provisions of animals that the public would enjoy looking at – many were donated by local residents.

Weekend promenaders by the bandstand, 1904. With restricted leisure time available, the man in the street looked to the local park for rest and recreation and a walk in the fresh air.

Clissold House reflected in the New River, 1905, reminds us of the select origins of this area of land. It was originally the estate of Jonathan Hoare of the banking family who built this classical villa.

Clissold Park, London, N: No. 3305

A questioning glance from a deer in the animal paddock in the 1920s. At this time there were five deer, a kangaroo, and a collection of rabbits. The collection varied over the years, but there was still a selection of animals here in the 1940s of a similar nature.

The shrubbery in 1908, with police for some reason lurking nearby. Surely nothing untoward is afoot in this respectable Edwardian suburb!

One of the two lakes in 1910. The western one has been used for boating at various times. There were also swans and ornamental ducks.

CLISSOLD PARK – THE MANSION, No.6.

Clissold House and driveway with the church beyond, 1912. The large villa with its six-reeded stone Doric columns was built by Joseph Woods for his uncle Jonathan Hoare, a merchant. It is a splendid but rather severe house with two storeys off the carriageway and three where it reaches ground level at the rear. The yellow bricks which are used were probably made of clay and chalk from the Thames Estuary area and carried by barge up the River Lea.

CLISSOLD PARK – STOKE NEWINGTON

Swans on the lake. The estate later became Crawshay's Farm being held by Mr Crawshay on a perpetual lease from the Ecclesiastical Commissioners at a fixed yearly rental of £109 and a fat turkey! Mrs Crawshay and her two daughters were regulars at the parish church, where the Revd Augustus Clissold was curate. Mr Crawshay was not happy when his elder daughter fell in love with the curate, and refused to consent to their marriage. However, after Crawshay's death the pair were married and he entered into a life possession of the property, his name becoming fixed as the name of the estate. On his death it reverted to the Crawshay family before being bought for the public after a campaign by John Runtz and Joseph Beck, and so it became Clissold Park rather than Crawshay Park.

Five

Albion Road
and Newington Green

The Rose & Crown public house as it was in 1806 – this ancient structure was pulled down in 1815. This, the original inn, stood back from the footway of Church Street. The replacement was painted by T.H. Shepherd in 1843, already looking quaint. Next to this inn in the 1820s, a new road was constructed over the fields of the Earl of Darlington's estate. Building plots were laid out along the line of way towards Newington Green. A large number of the plots were owned by Thomas Cubitt, who was just beginning to use his large-scale organisational methods for building large numbers of houses at one time. These Albion Road houses are the predecessors, therefore, of the later estates in places like Pimlico, Millbank, Clapham, Kemp Town, and Osborne on the Isle of Wight.

The Triangle, Albion Road, 1910. The sweep of Clissold Crescent, once Park Lane and also part of the development, veers off to the right out of the picture.

Albion Road, Stoke Newington

Looking down Albion Road towards Newington Green from near the Triangle, 1905. Shops have developed on the left to cater for local customers in this area.

Albion Road, 1907 style, with horse-bus service, front garden railings, and Sunday best dress.

1028. Albion Road. Stoke Newington

Leafy Albion Road with horse-bus, 1904. It seems the service was pretty frequent as it was often caught on camera.

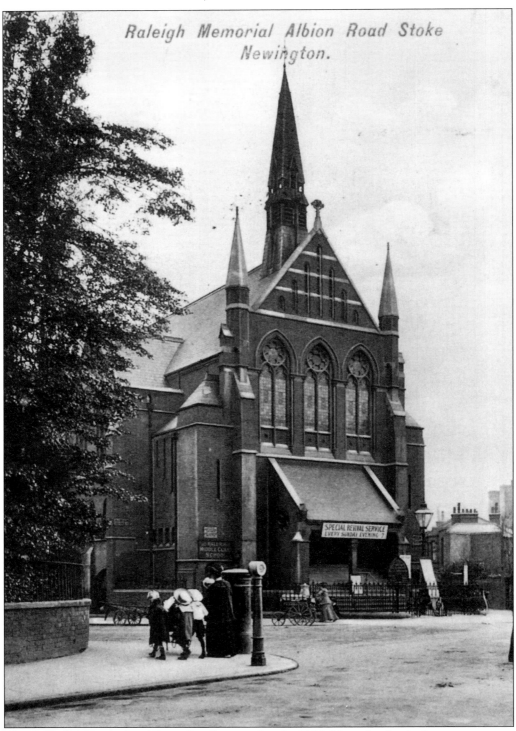

Raleigh Memorial Albion Road Stoke Newington.

The Raleigh Memorial – Albion Road's own church, 1904. Note the fire hydrant, a common piece of street furniture in pictures of this era.

A horse-bus crosses Green Lanes from Albion Road, making for the west side of Newington Green, 1905. Note the old chapel on the right.

Carysfort Road Stoke Newington.

Carysfort Road in 1906.

North- and south-facing views of Newington Green in 1824, when it was surrounded by cornfields and meadows.

As part of a commission, F.N. Shepherd recorded the appearance of Newington Green Chapel in the 1840s. This landmark of the area's Nonconformist traditions survived the demolition squads helping the Green to retain some of its old-world atmosphere into the twentieth century. Actually a very famous Unitarian meeting house, the building is dated 1708.

Metropolitan characteristics begin to show in Newington Green in the late nineteenth century, particularly tramlines for horsedrawn tramcars and fences around what had once been an unfenced green, in the middle. The upper storeys of London's earliest Georgian terrace still surviving, can be seen on the other side of the green (the darker elevation).

The south-east corner of the Green in 1909.

NEWINGTON GREEN.

A horse-tram negotiating the Green, 1905.

LONDON. Newington Green. No. 1006.

Under the trees at Newington Green.

Newington Green Road in 1905.

Newington Green traffic in 1928, looking west along Green Lanes.

The Life Saving Troop from Newington Green, 1934.

Six
Travelling to Town

The horse-tram en route for Newington Green in Green Lanes, near Petherton Road.

The Finsbury Park to Edmonton steam-tram, operated by the North London Suburban Tramway Co. Traffic was thin, so in January 1890 the operation was sold to the North Met which reverted to horse traction.

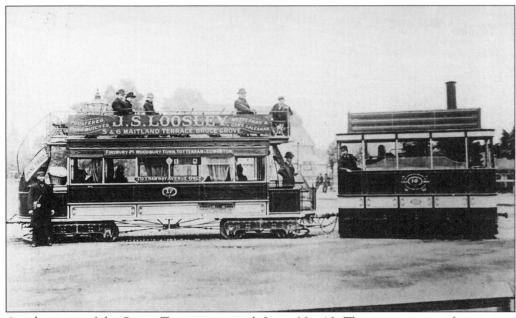

Another view of the Steam Tram service with Loco. No. 10. There were twenty-five engines and twenty-seven bogie cars to operate two lines from Stamford Hill to Ponders End and to Wood Green.

The early days of electric trams at the Finsbury Park terminus. The cars ran from here to Wood Green or Edmonton. The Methodist church can be seen in the distance. The Wood Green service began in July 1904.

A Stamford Hill tramway scene, 1907.

A Metropolitan Tram on route 27, with new trolleybus route 621, near the Manor House. The trees of Finsbury Park can be seen behind.

The Manor House hotel and early electric trams, 1904.

Manor House acquired a modern look when interchange islands were created to facilitate transfers between tramcar service and the underground railway. However, the Metropolitan Electric Trams, although part of the Underground group after 1914, were rather archaic in appearance until 1929, when a number of sleek 'Feltham' cars came into service.

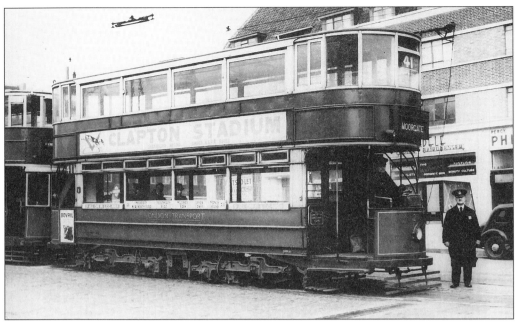

Around the corner from the Interchange at Manor House was the Green Lanes boarding point for Route 41 to Moorgate on the London County Council tram network. Trolleybuses later operated an extended route on this service.

In later London Transport days the 33 route used the same Green Lanes, Manor House terminus, running southwards via Newington Green and Stoke Newington's western boundary to the Kingsway Subway and South London.

The favourite horse-bus route between Stoke Newington and Victoria was a popular way of going into town. There were still many successful rivals to the giant London General Omnibus Company (L.G.O.C.) routes in the 1900s.

An L.G.O.C. vehicle running to London Bridge and the Elephant and Castle via Stoke Newington.

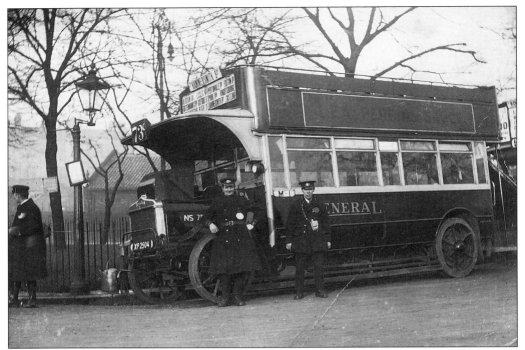

Into the petrol-driven era – a route 73c at Stoke Newington Common terminus. The N.S. type bus seen here was current between 1923 and 1937.

'B' Type bus 420 on route 67. The 'B's' were the first reliable mass-produced buses in London.

A 67-route photograph of a much later 'B' type (No. 4993) with cheerful conductor and driver. The type was current from 1910–1926 and was churned out from the L.G.O.C. workshops at Walthamstow, not very far away to the east of Stoke Newington.

All ready for a day's outing by 'General' bus in 1915. Many of the 'B' types were sent across to France to transport soldiers during the Great War.

Trolleybuses at the Manor House. The local tram routes were almost completely converted to overhead wire operation except for the No. 33 by the late 1930s.

Route 659 trolleybus at the Manor House. All the trolley routes were numbered in the 600s and 500s.

Seven

Around the Manor House

The old Manor House tavern flying its flag – it was not replaced by a new building until the 1930s, by which time the place had changed out of all recognition. Seven Sisters Road was not built until the mid-nineteenth century, while a tollgate guarded access to Green Lanes to the south.

The corner of Seven Sisters Road and Woodberry Down about 1906. Early maps mark the area as Berrie Down Wood.

Green Lanes, looking traffic-free in the 1920s with a car parked facing the wrong direction!

Manor House Tram Station.

Smart 'thirties design has transformed the Manor House crossroads with effective signposting complementing the tram interchange and rebuilt public house – the 'Underground' stylistic influence at its height.

At the northern edge of Stoke Newington, Northumberland House looks towards Hornsey Wood. It was built in 1822–4 and became a private asylum for the mentally sick. Gateposts at the entrance from Green Lanes were topped by the Percy family heraldic lion – these and the name are an allusion to a vague connection the builder had with the Earl of Northumberland.

The Hornsey Wood Tavern was an enormously popular leisure resort in the early nineteenth century, with its lakes, fields, and woodland. Finsbury Park was laid out over the site from 1869.

Eight

Green Lanes
and Highbury Borders

Houses like this one in Green Lanes had an impressive main floor approached by a flight of steps to the front door from the heavy wooden front garden gate, 1908.

The rather severe Brownswood Road houses in 1910.

On the edge of open spaces – Brownswood Park, Green Lanes in 1876.

The White House, Green Lanes, on the edge of the borough in about 1905.

Looking at the other side of the White House as seen from Highbury New Park in 1906 – a convenient place to drink when thirst overtook you while walking the dog in Clissold Park.

The route 33 tram stops for passengers near the White House, Green Lanes.

Once-secluded houses lay opposite the park behind stone gateways above the White House.

Green Lanes reaches a narrower section by Petherton Road where the New River dives underground by the church and Aden Terrace. In this part of Green Lanes there was a single track section of tram line, 1920.

Springdale Road with its trees led into the former Park Lane.

Park Lane was a quiet oasis in 1904. This lane was later renamed Clissold Crescent.

One of the most charming spots in Stoke Newington was this bridge over the New River in Park Lane.

New River follows its serpentine course by Park Lane.

Aden Grove, Green Lanes Stoke, Newington.

Aden Grove with its tall corner house, 1905. Note the children's dresses.

Over the border, Highbury New Park, with the church of St Augustine, retained a secluded air typical of streets adjacent to Parkland, 1904.

The Officer's Nursing Home, 118 Highbury New Park, in 1916. The Italianate villas were constructed in the mid-1850s along the wide roadway in which many large trees were planted.

Aberdeen Park in 1905. Built in 1853–4 and named after the Prime Minister of the day, the fourth Earl of Aberdeen. In December 1934 it was described as 'a quiet, secluded area where are to be found some of the biggest houses in Highbury with tennis courts – a refuge … and a joy in summer'.

St Paul's Road in 1906, which was once an ancient parish road known as Hopping Lane. In 1840, there were only three houses.

Shirley Hibbard's apiary at Stoke Newington, 1870. In 1874, she is recorded as living at Bridge House, Hermitage Road. Interested in natural history, she had noted in 1864 that the 'close cordon of bricks' beginning to surround part of the old village were 'threatening the local nightingales'.